Classic Guitars

Classic Guitars

by **robert shaw**

photographs by

michael tamborrino

Pomegranate
SAN FRANCISCO

Published by Pomegranate Communications, Inc.
Box 808022, Petaluma CA 94975
800 227 1428; www.pomegranate.com

Pomegranate Europe Ltd.
Unit 1, Heathcote Business Centre, Hurlbutt Road
Warwick, Warwickshire CV34 6TD, U. K.
[+44] 0 1926 430111

Library of Congress Cataloging-in-Publication Data
Shaw, Robert, 1951–
    Classic guitars / by Robert Shaw ; photographs by Michael Tamborrino.
        p. cm.
    Includes index.
    ISBN 0-7649-2888-0 (alk. paper)
     1. Guitar—Pictorial works. 2. Guitar. I. Tamborrino, Michael. II. Title.

ML1015.G9S51 2004
787.87'19—dc22   2004046506

Pomegranate Catalog No. A734

Designed by Harrah Lord, Yellow House Studio, Rockport, Maine
Printed in Korea

13 12 11 10 09 08 07 06 05 04   10 9 8 7 6 5 4 3 2 1

Introduction

This little book presents sixty-five of the most important and collectible guitars of the past two centuries. It includes guitars associated with a wide variety of musical styles, from genteel Victorian parlor music to crashing rock and roll, and the instruments illustrate the evolution of the guitar and the growth of its popularity and influence, from the 1830s to the present day.

Compared to the piano, the only instrument that can rival its versatility and popularity, the guitar is relatively simple to build. A single skilled craftsperson can design and create a high-quality guitar, whereas the production of a piano requires specialized resources and teamwork. The guitar is an extraordinarily malleable instrument, retaining its basic identity at the same time that it has allowed builders and players to achieve highly individual variations on its fundamental form and sound. With only six strings, the guitar is also relatively easy to play, and like a piano, it can provide both chords and single notes, accompanying a singer or carrying a solo with equal aplomb. Still more important, the guitar is easy to carry from place to place. It is a minstrel's instrument, and its portability has allowed it to travel the world, taking very different shapes and creating distinctive worlds of sound and attitude, from flamenco, tango, fado, and bossa nova to blues, country-western, slack key, and rock and roll.

All but a few of the guitars included in this book were made in the United

States, where the major modern innovations in guitar design have taken place and where most of the leading luthiers and manufacturers are located. But, like so many things that have become identified with America, the guitar came there from Europe, where it had been developed by skilled luthiers since the sixteenth century.

The guitar was a favorite in the courts and concert halls of Europe. Charles II of England and Louis XIV of France were both avid guitarists, and Benjamin Franklin played an English-made guitar. Antonio Stradivari made guitars as well as violins, and Hector Berlioz played a guitar given to him by Niccolò Paganini, a virtuoso on six strings as well as on the violin's four.

The first important American guitar maker, Christian Frederich Martin, came to New York from his native Saxony in 1833 and quickly established a thriving business in the city. His still prosperous C. F. Martin & Company is one of America's oldest continuously operating family businesses, and its acoustic flat-top guitars (and ukuleles) have long been considered the standard of excellence throughout the world.

During the nineteenth century, Martin's small-bodied instruments were most often played by women. The little instruments, which typically measured only 11 or 12 inches at their widest point, were strung with gut and used to play quiet, fashionable semiclassical waltzes and Spanish fandangos, or to accompany sentimental ballads and "heart" songs. As befitted his refined, urbane clientele, Martin often decorated his guitars with ivory and pearl inlay, creating instruments that were as pretty to look at as to hear.

American music began to change radically at the turn of the twentieth century, and the guitar was one of the major catalysts of change. Because they were expensive, guitars had largely been instruments for the well-to-do during the nineteenth century. Beginning in the 1890s, however, Sears Roebuck, Montgomery Ward, and other pioneer mail order catalog companies offered guitars for as little as $2; the instrument started to spread into the rural South and into the hands of untrained country musicians.

The guitar's great power and popularity have grown out of the meeting of European and African musical traditions in America. Guitars and guitarists played a pivotal role in the development of blues, country, bluegrass, and rock music and, although the instrument has been less important in jazz, such virtuoso jazz masters as Eddie Lang, Les Paul, Django Reinhardt, Charlie Christian, John McLaughlin, and Pat Metheny have exerted influence that has touched guitarists of all persuasions. All of these uniquely American forms of music have traveled around the world with the guitar and taken new shapes in other countries, as musicians have added their own cultural twists and traditions to the mix.

The years between the turn of the century and the early 1920s, when the first commercial recordings of blues, country, gospel and other "folk" music were made, were formative both for the music and the guitar's place within it. By the time the record companies sent talent scouts to the South to begin their ventures in "race" (i.e., music by and for poor Southern blacks) and "hillbilly" (i.e., music by and for poor Southern whites) recordings, the guitar had assumed a central role in American popular music. It had become the people's instrument. That role was solidified and expanded by the phonograph record, which put thousands of recordings of blues and country guitarists into the hands of aspiring musicians in the 1920s and 1930s. In the late twenties, the guitar-driven music of the Carter family and Jimmie Rodgers defined country music, while recordings of seminal blues guitarists like Charlie Patton, Blind Lemon Jefferson, Blind Blake, and Blind Willie Johnson set the standards for all subsequent pickers.

Paralleling the rise of American popular music, American guitar makers have dominated guitar design since the late nineteenth century, providing most of the innovations adopted by luthiers and manufacturers in other countries over the past hundred years. During this time, the American concerns C. F. Martin,

Gibson, and Fender redefined the way guitars were designed and built, finding ways to produce large numbers of high-quality instruments, while individual American artisans such as John D'Angelico, Elmer Stromberg, and James D'Aquisto have, along with the often anonymous master craftsmen working for large companies like Martin, Epiphone, and Gibson, set the standards for modern guitar craftsmanship.

In many ways, the story of the guitar in the twentieth century has been about the search for greater volume. Performers looked for instruments that could be heard above the din of a crowd, or cut through a jazz band's horn section. Guitar makers tried a variety of strategies to pump up the volume. Heavily braced, steel-stringed instruments were introduced around 1904, and the louder, more percussive, more versatile sound of steel slowly began to eclipse the genteel gut that had been favored in the previous century. In Michigan, Orville Gibson produced the first archtops: guitars with a hand-carved convex top like that of a violin or cello. In the 1930s, the bodies of archtop and flattop guitars ballooned to great size, with lower bouts growing to 17, 18, or even 19 inches wide. Guitars with metal bodies and interior resonators were introduced by the Dopyera brothers, and Los Angeles guitar builder Hermann Weissenborn hollowed out the necks of his Hawaiian guitars to provide a larger resonating chamber. Finally, in the mid-thirties, experiments with electric amplification began the transition that would transform the guitar into the loudest of instruments.

The first electrics were small-bodied lap steels, made to amplify the popular sound of Hawaiian slide guitar. The little solid-bodied instruments were played flat in the lap with a steel slide. Guitar virtuoso Les Paul, who was among the pioneers of the electric guitar, realized that solid-bodied instruments, which would not resonate and feed back when amplified, were the wave of the future; he began experimenting with full-sized solid-bodied guitars in the late 1930s. To prove his point, he mounted electric pickups and a bridge on a length of four-by-four, attached a neck (and two halves of a hollowbody so it looked more like a conventional instrument), and in 1941 took his "Log" to the Gibson company. Paul was too far ahead of his time, however, and the concept would not reach consumers for nearly another decade.

In 1950, a California inventor named Leo Fender introduced the first commercially viable solid-bodied electric guitar; he followed it in 1951 with an even more radical and original instrument, a solid-bodied electric bass guitar. Fender's simple, affordable guitars changed popular music forever, and his revolutionary Telecaster and Stratocaster models are still made and widely played today. Seeing Fender's success, Gibson quickly got back in touch with Les Paul. The first solid-bodied Gibson, the Les Paul Model, was introduced in mid-1952.

Leo Fender designed his guitars with Western swing players in mind, but they were soon picked up by early rockers like Buddy Holly and Richie Valens. Whether solid- or hollow-bodied, the new electric guitars' loud cutting sound defined the sound of rock and roll, and their bold, sleek styling only added to the anarchic menace of the new music.

The folk music boom of the late fifties and early sixties brought the rural guitar sounds of the twenties and thirties to mass culture; the British invasion a few years later sealed the bargain, taking the guitar to new heights of popularity. By the mid-sixties, it seemed as if everyone either played guitar or knew someone who did. The instrument became a tool and symbol of the profound cultural changes that swept the Western world in the 1960s.

Today, there are more skilled craftsmen making guitars than at any time in history. The nearly moribund archtop tradition has been rejuvenated by luthiers such as James D'Aquisto and John Monteleone. Designers like Ken Parker and Paul Reed Smith continue to expand and refine the capabilities of electric instruments, and dozens of flattop builders are making instruments that rival the finest prewar Martins and Gibsons. Baby boomers are buying the guitars they could not afford as kids, and prices for the most coveted vintage instruments have reached five and even six figures. As a new millennium begins, the 500-year-old guitar continues to mature and adapt to shifts in the culture and popular taste. It seems sure to be with us for many, many years to come.

· · · · ·

Curator, musician, and art historian Robert Shaw has written extensively on American music and folk art. His books include *America's Traditional Crafts, Quilts: A Living Tradition, American Baskets,* and *Great Guitars.* With Michael Tamborrino, he has produced a calendar, *Classic Guitars,* for Pomegranate since 1999.

Michael Tamborrino is a photographer, writer, artist, and musician whose work has appeared in *Acoustic Guitar, Guitar Player,* and many other publications. Currently a member of the New York Press Photographers Association, he has also been an executive board member of the American Society of Media Photographers.

ClassicGuitars

Martin presentation guitar, 1834

CHRISTIAN FRIEDRICH MARTIN SR. / C. F. MARTIN & CO. / NEW YORK, NEW YORK / THE CHINERY COLLECTION

Christian Friedrich Martin Sr. (1796–1873) learned carpentry and guitar making from his father; he later worked for the renowned Vienna violin maker and luthier Johann Georg Stauffer, serving him as foreman for a number of years.

During his early years in America, Martin made guitars for upper-class New Yorkers who could afford the finest materials and decorative inlay work. The unique, custom-made presentation guitar shown here has an elephant ivory fingerboard, headstock, and bridge, while its body and sound hole are inlaid with half-moons of abalone and ivory.

Martin parlor guitar with coffin case, c. 1890

C. F. MARTIN & CO. / NAZARETH, PENNSYLVANIA / PRIVATE COLLECTION

Beginning in the 1850s, C. F. Martin moved away from the influence of the German guitar-making tradition he had grown up with and created the first truly American guitars. The beautifully proportioned body forms and elegant but restrained decorative styles that he developed have set the standard for all subsequent flattop guitar makers.

Early Martin guitars came with a high-quality, plush-lined wooden case, now often referred to as a "coffin case" by collectors for its distinctive shape.

Archtop guitar, c. 1900

ORVILLE H. GIBSON / KALAMAZOO, MICHIGAN / GIBSON GUITAR CORPORATION, NASHVILLE, TENNESSEE

$\mathcal{O}rville$ H. Gibson (1856–1918) was one of the most innovative and influential fretted-instrument designers of all time. His mandolin designs are still the standard by which all other mandolins are judged, and he is generally recognized as the father of the archtop guitar.

Gibson revolutionized fretted-instrument design by applying violin-making techniques to the luthier's craft. Because he thought bending wood into shape deadened its tone, he carved the tops and backs of his mandolins and guitars and sawed the rims from solid blocks of wood. In the early decades of the twentieth century, the Gibson company built on his prototypes to become the leading manufacturer of archtop mandolins and guitars.

Gibson Style 0 Harp Guitar, c. 1915

GIBSON GUITAR CORPORATION / KALAMAZOO, MICHIGAN / PRIVATE COLLECTION

Although it is little more than a historical curiosity today, the harp guitar was considered the cutting edge of guitar design in the early years of the twentieth century. Harp guitars combined a standard six-string guitar neck with six to twelve sub-bass "harp" strings set off the neck. The additional strings could not be fretted but allowed players to add deep bass notes to chords fingered on the neck. Primarily associated with light classical music, harp guitars remained popular through the teens but quickly fell from favor in the fast-changing Jazz Age years.

Gibson was the leading manufacturer of harp guitars, offering two models from its earliest years into the late 1930s, long after demand or even interest had waned.

Prairie State, c. 1935 / Euphonon, 1939 / W. J. Dyer & Bro.
Symphony No. 8 harp guitar, c. 1920

CARL AND AUGUST LARSON / CHICAGO, ILLINOIS / THE CHINERY COLLECTION

Because they did not make instruments under their own name, the Swedish-born Larson brothers are not well known today. They were, however, among the most prolific and innovative luthiers of the early twentieth century. The Larsons were the first significant makers of steel-stringed flattop guitars, and their varied and highly original output of fretted instruments rivals those of the Martin and Gibson companies.

The Prairie State is one of the largest acoustic guitars ever made, with a massive 21-inch lower bout. The Symphony is generally considered to be the most playable harp guitar ever built and is favored by many contemporary guitarists over Gibson's much more common and familiar models.

Style 3 Hawaiian guitar, c. 1930

ATTRIBUTED TO HERMANN WEISSENBORN
LOS ANGELES, CALIFORNIA
PRIVATE COLLECTION

Hermann Weissenborn invented a guitar designed specifically for Hawaiian slide playing. Weissenborn's guitars had thin bodies (since Hawaiian players laid their instruments flat in their laps and fretted them with a steel bar), frets that were flush with the fingerboard rather than slightly raised (so the steel bar wouldn't produce unwanted clacking noises as it traveled up and down the strings), and thick square necks that were hollowed out to produce incredible sustain. He is believed to have made a variety of models that were marketed under different brand names, and his fancier styles featured rope binding. Weissenborn guitars have been championed in recent years by the great slide player David Lindley.

National Resonator Guitars: Style O, 1930 (left) and DON, 1934

NATIONAL STRING INSTRUMENT CORPORATION / LOS ANGELES, CALIFORNIA / PRIVATE COLLECTION

$\mathcal{M}$*any* different approaches to increasing volume were tried in the days before electric guitars. National's Style O guitar featured a large single resonator that amplified the instrument's sound for more volume. Its brass body was plated with nickel and decorated with exotic sandblasted tropical designs.

Resonator guitars produced an extremely loud, metallic sound that found special favor with Hawaiian and blues guitarists in the late 1920s and early 1930s. The company claimed their instruments were seven times louder than conventional acoustics. The Dobro played by bluegrass musicians is a variation of the single-resonator guitar with a wooden body.

Selmer/Maccaferri guitars, c. 1932–1933

SELMER MUSICAL INSTRUMENT COMPANY / PARIS, FRANCE / THE CHINERY COLLECTION

These three subtle variations on a theme were designed by the Italian instrument maker and concert guitarist Mario Maccaferri for the Selmer instrument company of Paris. Maccaferri (1900–1993), a colleague of Andrés Segovia, built a considerable reputation in Europe in the 1920s for his classical recitals. The upper bouts of Maccaferri's guitars were "cut away," allowing the player to reach the upper frets more easily, and they featured a novel "floating" soundboard inside to offset the loss of resonance caused when the player's body touched the back of the guitar.

The Selmer/Maccaferri guitar is closely associated with the legendary Belgian Gypsy guitarist Django Reinhardt, best known for his work with violinist Stephane Grappelli and the Hot Club of Paris. Reinhardt's lyrical, passionate, swinging style, accomplished with two fingers of a fire-crippled left hand, has influenced guitarists as diverse as Les Paul, Chet Atkins, and B. B. King.

Gibson Super 400PN, 1939, and Super 400, 1934

GIBSON GUITAR CORPORATION / KALAMAZOO, MICHIGAN / THE CHINERY COLLECTION

When it was introduced in 1934, the Gibson Super 400 (right) was the biggest, fanciest, and most expensive archtop ever built. It set a lofty new standard for archtop guitar making, and inspired all of Gibson's competitors to produce instruments of similar or even greater size and quality. In 1939, Gibson followed the Super 400's success with the Super 400 Premier, which added a right-hand cutaway to the upper bout and could be special-ordered in a handsome blonde finish.

The Super 400 is one of the most influential guitar designs of all time. It inspired some of the finest fretted instruments ever made, including John D'Angelico's New Yorker and Elmer Stromberg's Master 400—both, along with vintage Super 400s, among the most magnificent, highly valued, and respected of all American guitars.

Rickenbacker Electro-Spanish, c. 1935

ELECTRO STRING INSTRUMENT CORPORATION / LOS ANGELES, CALIFORNIA / PRIVATE COLLECTION

This rare little instrument is a cousin of electric Hawaiian lap-style guitars and one of the first electric guitars offered commercially. Hawaiian music was wildly popular throughout the 1930s, and Hawaiian slide guitars were featured in many country and pop records of the era. This three-quarter-size guitar was made to be fretted and played conventionally, in so-called "Spanish" style, rather than flat in the lap. It was briefly used by a few pioneering guitarists, including Eldon Shamblin of Bob Wills's Texas Playboys. Wills spoke for many when he told Shamblin to put it away because audiences wanted to see people playing "real" guitars.

Martin 000-45, c. 1939

C. F. MARTIN & CO. / NAZARETH, PENNSYLVANIA / PRIVATE COLLECTION

With a less bass-heavy sound than the company's slightly larger Dreadnoughts, Martin's 000 size has been a favorite of fingerpickers for many years. The fancy Style 45, with extensive pearl and abalone inlay, was Martin's top of the line from 1902 until 1942, when it was discontinued. The model was reintroduced in 1968, and Martin continues to make a few Style 45s each year. This guitar has 14 frets clear of the body, a rare variation that was introduced in 1934. Only 123 14-fret 000-45s were made between 1934 and 1942.

Gibson Super Jumbo-100 (left) and Super Jumbo-200, 1939

GIBSON GUITAR COMPANY / KALAMAZOO, MICHIGAN / PRIVATE COLLECTION

Among the biggest movie stars of the 1930s, singing cowboys such as Gene Autrey and Ray Whitley helped to popularize the guitar as an instrument to accompany singing. The first Super Jumbo was made for Whitley, who provided Gibson with his ideas for a big, fancy western-style guitar with a booming bass sound. After Whitley played it on camera, a Super Jumbo became every young cowboy's dream.

Stromberg Master 400 and Master 300, c. 1950

CHARLES A. STROMBERG AND SON / BOSTON, MASSACHUSETTS / PRIVATE COLLECTION

Elmer Stromberg, the son in the firm Charles A. Stromberg and Son, created some of the finest archtop jazz guitars ever made. Modeled after Gibson's Super 400, his top-of-the-line Master 400 was even bigger and louder than its inspiration and competitor. A number of big-band guitarists, including Count Basie's Freddy Green and Duke Ellington's Fred Guy, chose the Stromberg because its cutting tone and enormous volume allowed it to be heard even through a large horn section.

Leilani lap steel guitar and amp, c. 1955

GORLEY CO. / SANTA MONICA, CALIFORNIA / PRIVATE COLLECTION

Because they were small and lay flat in the lap when played, solid-bodied Hawaiian lap steels could take on many unusual forms and support diverse decorative treatments. This coordinated guitar-and-amp set is covered with pearloid, a shiny synthetic that was also popular on drum sets in the 1950s.

Fender Telecaster (c. 1952, left) and Telecaster Custom, 1959

FENDER MUSICAL INSTRUMENT COMPANY / FULLERTON, CALIFORNIA / PRIVATE COLLECTION

The Fender Telecaster revolutionized electric guitar design and remains one of the icons of blues, country, and rock and roll. Its biting, trebly tone has been favored by such distinctive stylists as James Burton, Albert Collins, Roy Buchanan, Steve Cropper, Robbie Robertson, and Keith Richards, and Bruce Springsteen's favorite electric is a vintage Esquire, a single-pickup version of the Tele. The inexpensive, no-frills guitar originally came only in a plain blonde finish; the sunburst Custom was introduced in 1959.

Fender Precision bass guitars, c. 1952–1960

FENDER MUSICAL INSTRUMENT COMPANY / FULLERTON, CALIFORNIA / PRIVATE COLLECTION

In addition to introducing the first commercially successful solid-bodied electric guitars, Leo Fender was also first with the even more revolutionary electric bass guitar. It was quickly adopted by country and rock musicians, who found it louder, easier to play, and far more portable than the upright bass fiddles it replaced. The Fender bass helped to define the sound of rock and roll and modern country music in the 1950s and 1960s. With the Telecaster and Stratocaster, it is among the most widely copied instrument designs of all time.

Gibson Les Paul "Gold Tops." Left: 1952; right: c. 1953–1955

GIBSON GUITAR CORPORATION / KALAMAZOO, MICHIGAN / PRIVATE COLLECTION

The legendary Les Paul championed the idea of solid-bodied electric guitars long before they became commercially viable. Although Gibson had no interest when Paul first approached them about building solid-bodied guitars, they enlisted his advice and endorsement soon after the introduction of the Fender Telecaster in 1950. The Les Paul, featuring a gold single-cutaway body, was introduced in 1952. To make it look and sound different from a Fender, Gibson laminated a carved maple top onto a flat mahogany body.

Fender Stratocaster, c. 1954

FENDER MUSICAL INSTRUMENT COMPANY / FULLERTON, CALIFORNIA / PRIVATE COLLECTION

The Fender Stratocaster is the king of rock-and-roll guitars, played by everyone from Buddy Holly to Stevie Ray Vaughan since its introduction in 1954. The versatile Strat's toggle switch allows the three pickups to be mixed in different tonal combinations and its optional vibrato bar has been used to great effect by the likes of pioneer surf guitarist Dick Dale and the inimitable Jimi Hendrix.

This early sunburst Strat originally sold for $324, a price any guitarist would be more than happy to ante up today. Vintage Stratocasters in good condition can now bring more than fifty times that original price.

Gretsch White Penguin and Chet Atkins 6120, c. 1954

FRED GRETSCH MANUFACTURING COMPANY / NEW YORK, NEW YORK / PRIVATE COLLECTION

The Gretsch company, founded in 1883 by German immigrant Friedrich Gretsch to build drums, tambourines, and banjos, is one of America's largest and oldest instrument manufacturers. Although it is best known for its superb drums, the company expanded into guitars in the 1920s and produced a number of classic electrics in the 1950s. These two guitars represent the top of the company's solid- and hollow-bodied lines; they were especially popular with country and rockabilly players of the time. Associated with Gretsch for many years, Nashville master Chet Atkins designed a number of instruments that bear his name.

Gretsch White Falcon, c. 1955

FRED GRETSCH MANUFACTURING CO. / NEW YORK, NEW YORK / PRIVATE COLLECTION

With a list price of $600 in 1955, the hollow-bodied White Falcon was far and away the most expensive electric guitar of its time. The Falcon certainly made a statement: it was huge, measuring 17 inches across the lower bout, and came replete with glittering gold binding and pick guard, elaborately engraved fingerboard inlays, and rhinestone-tipped control knobs. Originally made as a one-of-a-kind showpiece for a trade show, the White Falcon caused such a stir that Gretsch decided to market it. While its price and size kept it from the popularity of less expensive Fender and Gibson electrics, the White Falcon has always had its champions (notably Neil Young and Stephen Stills), while for collectors it remains the most prized of all Gretsch models.

Gretsch Round-Up, c. 1955

FRED GRETSCH MANUFACTURING CO. / NEW YORK, NEW YORK / PRIVATE COLLECTION

The solid-bodied Round-Up was introduced in 1954, at the height of a craze for western movies and clothing. The richly decorated guitar featured a branded G, tooled leather side trim, a cowboy belt buckle below its bridge, and Western motifs on its pegboard, fingerboard, and pick guard.

Gibson Flying V, 1958

GIBSON GUITAR CORPORATION / KALAMAZOO, MICHIGAN / PRIVATE COLLECTION

Although Gibson introduced the solid-bodied Les Paul in 1952, company president Ted McCarty soon realized that he had to do something really different and forward-looking to modernize the company's image and compete successfully with Fender.

Because the whole aim of a solid-bodied guitar is to produce sound strictly through the interaction of vibrating strings and electric pickups—with no resonant contribution from the body—its shape need not be constrained to follow traditional forms. In 1957, McCarty designed several radically shaped instruments with the help of a local artist. This one was intended to look like an arrow, but someone in the company said it looked like a flying v, and the name stuck. Although the Flying V was a flop when first released, such sixties masters as Lonnie Mack and Dave Davies of the Kinks brought it into fashion, and Gibson began manufacturing reissues of the model in 1967.

The angular, lightning bolt–shaped Explorer and its sister model, the Flying V, were the first solid-bodied electric guitars to completely break away from the curved forms of traditional fretted instruments. These radical designs proved too far ahead of their time: both instruments were commercial failures. They set the stage for many later and even wilder experiments with body shapes, however, and have become collectors' items that sell well into five figures. Fewer than twenty-five Explorers are believed to have been produced in the model's two-year production run, making it among the rarest of all American guitars.

Fender Stratocaster, c. 1957

FENDER MUSICAL INSTRUMENT COMPANY / FULLERTON, CALIFORNIA / PRIVATE COLLECTION

This rare deluxe Strat is nicknamed "Mary Kaye" by collectors, after the otherwise forgotten entertainer who posed with it in Fender's late-1950s catalogs. The elegant instrument features a custom blonde finish through which the grain of the ash body can be seen.

Gibson ES-335TN (1959, left), ES-335TN (1959), and ES-335TDC, 1963

GIBSON GUITAR COMPANY / KALAMAZOO, MI / PRIVATE COLLECTION

Introduced in 1958, the Gibson ES-335 attempted to combine the best qualities of hollow- and solid-bodied electrics in a single instrument. The new guitar quickly became popular with jazz, blues, and rock players, being versatile enough to suit their differing needs. The ES-335 is most closely identified with B. B. King, whose Gibson hollowbodies, all named "Lucille," are almost as well known as he is.

Fender Stratocasters, c. 1961

FENDER ELECTRIC INSTRUMENT CO. / FULLERTON, CALIFORNIA / PRIVATE COLLECTION

Although the Stratocaster's standard color has always been a brown sunburst, other finishes such as the "Mary Kaye" white were available by special order in the 1950s. Fender officially widened options in 1961, when the company advertised a palette of fourteen custom colors. All three of these custom-colored Strats lack the model's standard tremolo unit, a variation collectors call "hard-tail."

The Stratocaster is the most widely imitated guitar design of all time. Strat copies have been made by dozens of companies around the world; Fender itself now offers inexpensive versions made in Mexico and Korea, as well as expensive reproductions of classic early variations.

Hoyer Bianka, 1961

HOYER INSTRUMENT COMPANY
TENNENLOHE, GERMANY
THE CHINERY COLLECTION

Rock and roll became popular in Germany during the 1950s, when thousands of American GIs (including Elvis Presley) were stationed there. In the early sixties, many of the bands that would launch the British Invasion honed their craft playing in rough-and-tumble German clubs.

Hoyer was one of several German manufacturers to make guitars that were more affordable than imported Fenders and Gibsons. This elaborately carved and inlaid hollow-bodied electric represents the best in German-made guitars of the era.

Hofner 500/1 "Violin" bass guitars, c. 1961–1963

HOFNER MUSICAL INSTRUMENT COMPANY / BUBENREUTH, GERMANY / PRIVATE COLLECTION

The violin-shaped Hofner bass guitar is nicknamed "the Beatle bass" because its best-known player is Paul McCartney. Many other British Invasion bassists also used the Hofner, which they discovered while playing clubs in Hamburg, Germany. The Hofner was significantly cheaper than imported Fender basses, and its hollow body produced a sound more like that of an acoustic bass than the solid-bodied Fenders. In McCartney's imaginative hands, that sound became an integral part of the Beatles' magic.

Rickenbacker 360-12, c. 1965

RICKENBACKER, INC. / LOS ANGELES, CALIFORNIA / COLLECTION OF CRAIG BRODY

The twelve-stringed Rickenbacker 360-12 was introduced in 1964 by Beatle George Harrison, who used it to create the distinctive opening chord of " A Hard Day's Night"; he also played it on "You Can't Do That." Recognizing that the odd-looking guitar's tone was a perfect complement to his group's developing sound, Jim (Roger) McGuinn of the Byrds got a guitar like Harrison's and became the instrument's champion and master. The jangly, chiming sound of McGuinn's Rickenbacker twelve-string defined folk-rock on such mid-sixties classics as "Mr. Tambourine Man," "Turn, Turn, Turn," and "Eight Miles High."

Vox Phantom Guitar Organ and Phantom XII, c. 1966

VOX INSTRUMENT COMPANY / LONDON, ENGLAND / PRIVATE COLLECTION

Vox's teardrop-shaped Phantom guitars were first seen in the hands of British Invasion players such as the Pretty Things and Brian Jones of the Rolling Stones. The Vox guitar organ was a rather bizarre and short-lived attempt to combine the two instruments. The frets were connected to organ tone generators so that when the instrument was fretted, it produced electric-organ sounds rather than normal guitar tones.

Fender Telecasters, c. 1968

FENDER MUSICAL INSTRUMENT COMPANY / FULLERTON, CALIFORNIA / PRIVATE COLLECTION

In 1968, at the height of "flower power," Fender introduced two new finishes for its Telecaster—pink paisley and floral blue. Neither proved very popular, and the psychedelic finishes were discontinued after 1969. James Burton, who played guitar for Elvis for years, still plays a paisley Tele and says the King loved the way the guitar looked. Because few were made, the instruments are rare and eagerly sought by collectors as nostalgic period pieces.

D'Aquisto New Yorkers, 1968–1969

JAMES D'AQUISTO / HUNTINGTON, NEW YORK / PRIVATE COLLECTION

James D'Aquisto apprenticed with the great New York luthier John D'Angelico in the mid-1950s, and he kept the art of the archtop alive almost single-handedly after his mentor's death in 1964. D'Aquisto provided the bridge between D'Angelico and the new generation of archtop builders who began work in the seventies and eighties. More than a few experts rank him as the greatest guitar craftsman of all time. He has exerted a profound influence on the many extraordinary artisans working with the archtop form today, including John Monteleone and Robert Benedetto.

The New Yorker was John D'Angelico's signature model, which D'Aquisto mastered and later modified as he pursued his own muse. These two guitars are examples of his early work, still very much in the D'Angelico tradition.

Gibson "The Les Paul," c. 1976

GIBSON INC. / NASHVILLE, TENNESSEE / PRIVATE COLLECTION

Gibson discontinued the original carved-top Les Paul in 1961, but it was redis-covered by sixties guitar gods like Mike Bloomfield, Eric Clapton, Jeff Beck, and Jimmy Page and reintroduced in the late 1960s. This ornate limited-edition Les Paul has a tiger-stripe maple top, back, and neck, gold-plated metal parts, and ebony knobs, bindings, and pick guard. Gibson continues to make a variety of Les Pauls today.

Abel Axe, c. 1994

ABEL AXE LLC / EVANSTON, WYOMING / PRIVATE COLLECTION

The innovative Abel Axe featured a solid aluminum body drilled with numerous beveled holes. The exceptionally dense body, which is only one inch thick, gives these guitars incredible sustain and unique sound qualities that some players rave about. They were not commercially successful, however, and only about two hundred were made between 1994 and 1996.

Krawczak Topcover Acoustic Guitar Model 3, 1994

KRAWCZAK GUITARS / WARWICK, RHODE ISLAND / PRIVATE COLLECTION

Kazimierz Krawczak's topcover acoustic represents a complete rethinking of acoustic principles. The topcover guitar has two spruce soundboards, each of which is recessed into the body. The upper soundboard can be seen through the extraordinarily large sound hole. The guitar is enormous, measuring 19 inches at the lower bout, as large as the biggest acoustics ever made by D'Angelico, Gibson, or Stromberg. The highly polished, oiled wood surface combines a jointed cherry top and back with laminated walnut sides and a maple neck.

Paul Reed Smith Artist 6/12 doubleneck, c. 1995

PAUL REED SMITH GUITARS / ANNAPOLIS, MARYLAND / PRIVATE COLLECTION

Double-necked electric guitars, which offer players two different string configurations on a single body, have been made since the 1950s. Like this example, most have a six-string and a twelve-string neck, allowing the player to switch back and forth without changing instruments.

Paul Reed Smith has been designing and manufacturing his highly regarded guitars since 1984. They combine the sound and feel of the two iconic solid-bodied electrics—the Fender Stratocaster and the Gibson Les Paul—with innovative modern design elements and electronics.

Paul Reed Smith Dragon, 1995

PAUL REED SMITH GUITARS
ANNAPOLIS, MARYLAND
PRIVATE COLLECTION

Paul Reed Smith introduced his first solid-bodied electric guitar, the Paul Reed Smith Custom, in 1984. Since then his fastidiously crafted guitars, made in a small factory in Annapolis, have achieved the status of modern classics. Played by such well-known musicians as Carlos Santana, Al Di Meola, and Dicky Betts, they are compared favorably with the vintage Stratocasters and Les Pauls that originally inspired Smith both as a musician and as a luthier.

This limited-edition guitar is the fanciest and most expensive made by the Paul Reed Smith company.

A Dragon in the collection of the Smithsonian Institution's National Museum of American History was included in the museum's 1994 exhibition "The Guitar in American Popular Music."

Blue Guitars by (left to right)
James D'Aquisto, John Monteleone, and Robert Bennedetto

1994 (D'AQUISTO), 1996 (OTHERS) / THE CHINERY COLLECTION

In 1995, the late collector Scott Chinery commissioned twenty-one of the world's finest luthiers to each craft a single-cutaway archtop guitar. Beyond the body style, only two specifications were given to the craftspeople: that the guitar measure eighteen inches across its lower bout and that it be finished in blue to match a guitar (above left) built for Chinery by James D'Aquisto. The resulting Blue Guitars testify to the skill and imagination of the many contemporary luthiers who have brought the archtop to an unprecedented level of sophistication and technical innovation in recent years.

James D'Aquisto's Blue Guitar, the Centura Deluxe, was one of the last instruments he made before his death in 1995, and the series stands, at least in part, as a tribute to his enduring artistry and influence.

Parker Fly Deluxe, 1996

PARKER GUITARS / WILMINGTON, MASSACHUSETTS

Introduced commercially in 1994, the Parker Fly represents the first complete redesign of the six-string electric guitar since the Fender Telecaster appeared more than forty years before. The revolutionary Fly, which incorporates a number of new design, technology, and manufacturing process patents, was developed over the course of nine years of experimentation by master craftsman Ken Parker and electronics wizard Larry Fishman.

A space-age skin of carbon and glass fiber bonded with epoxy resin keeps the Fly's extremely thin and lightweight poplar body and basswood neck from being torn apart by string tension. Fishman combined magnetic and bridge-mounted piezoelectric pickups on the guitar, enabling it to create both a typical range of electric sounds and a realistic amplified-acoustic sound. Fishman's system also allows the player to blend the two types of sounds, effectively making the Fly two instruments at once.

Although traditionalists like Keith Richards won't play it on stage, Richards and many other guitarists, including Eddie van Halen and U2's The Edge, were quick to recognize and take advantage of the Fly's unique sound capabilities.

Monteleone Grand Artist Triport Deluxe, c. 1998

JOHN MONTELEONE / ISLIP, NEW YORK / PRIVATE COLLECTION

Acoustic jazz guitars with carved convex (arched) tops are very difficult to make and have long been considered the pinnacle of the luthier's art. John Monteleone has been building archtops for more than thirty years; he is widely regarded as one of the reigning masters of the form, and his guitars (and mandolins) are coveted by players and collectors around the world. This remarkable example of his work features a Monteleone innovation: two sound holes on the top side that project sound toward the player.

Index